I am a Giraffe

Aaron Carr

www.av2books.com

MEDIA ENHANCED BOOKS
AV² BY WEIGL™
ADDED VALUE • AUDIO VISUAL

Go to **www.av2books.com**, and enter this book's unique code.

BOOK CODE

A158067

AV² by Weigl brings you media enhanced books that support active learning.

AV² provides enriched content that supplements and complements this book. Weigl's AV² books strive to create inspired learning and engage young minds in a total learning experience.

Your AV² Media Enhanced books come alive with...

Audio
Listen to sections of the book read aloud.

Video
Watch informative video clips.

Embedded Weblinks
Gain additional information for research.

Try This!
Complete activities and hands-on experiments.

Key Words
Study vocabulary, and complete a matching word activity.

Quizzes
Test your knowledge.

Slide Show
View images and captions, and prepare a presentation.

... and much, much more!

Published by AV² by Weigl
350 5th Avenue, 59th Floor New York, NY 10118
Website: www.av2books.com   www.weigl.com

Library of Congress Cataloguing in Publication data available upon request.
Fax 1-866-449-3445 for the attention of the Publishing Records department.

ISBN 978-1-62127-282-3 (hardcover)
ISBN 978-1-62127-288-5 (softcover)

Printed in the United States of America in North Mankato, Minnesota
1 2 3 4 5 6 7 8 9 0 17 16 15 14 13

022013
WEP300113

Senior Editor: Aaron Carr   Art Director: Terry Paulhus

Weigl acknowledges Getty Images as the primary image supplier for this title.

I am a Giraffe

In this book, I will teach you about

- myself
- my food
- my home
- my family

and much more!

I am a giraffe.

I am the tallest animal in the world.

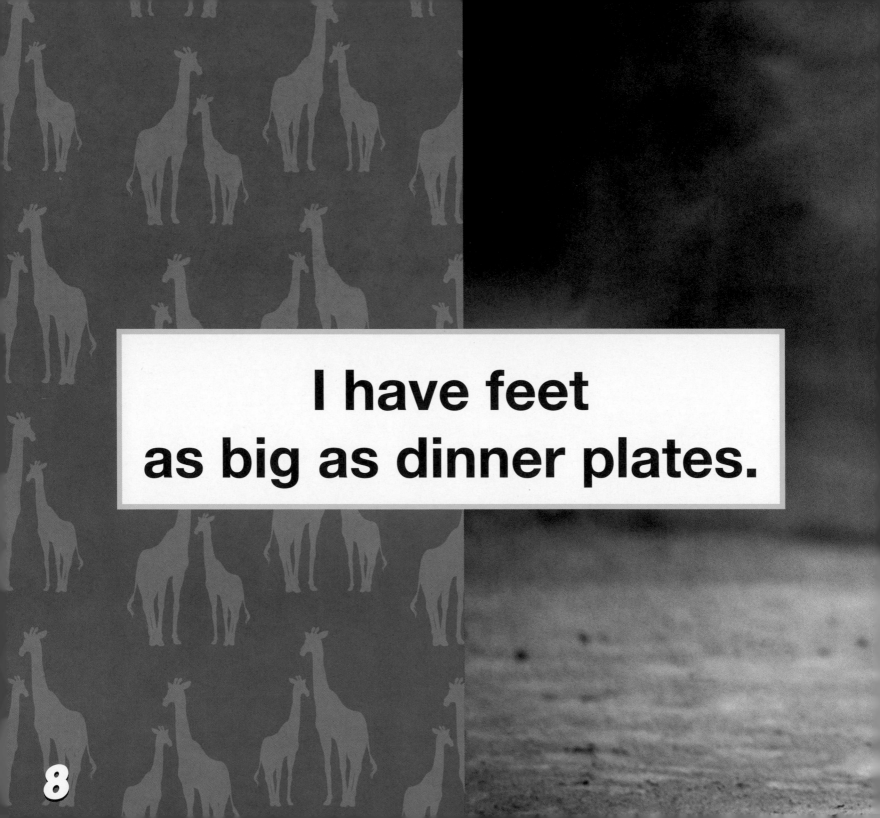

I have feet
as big as dinner plates.

8

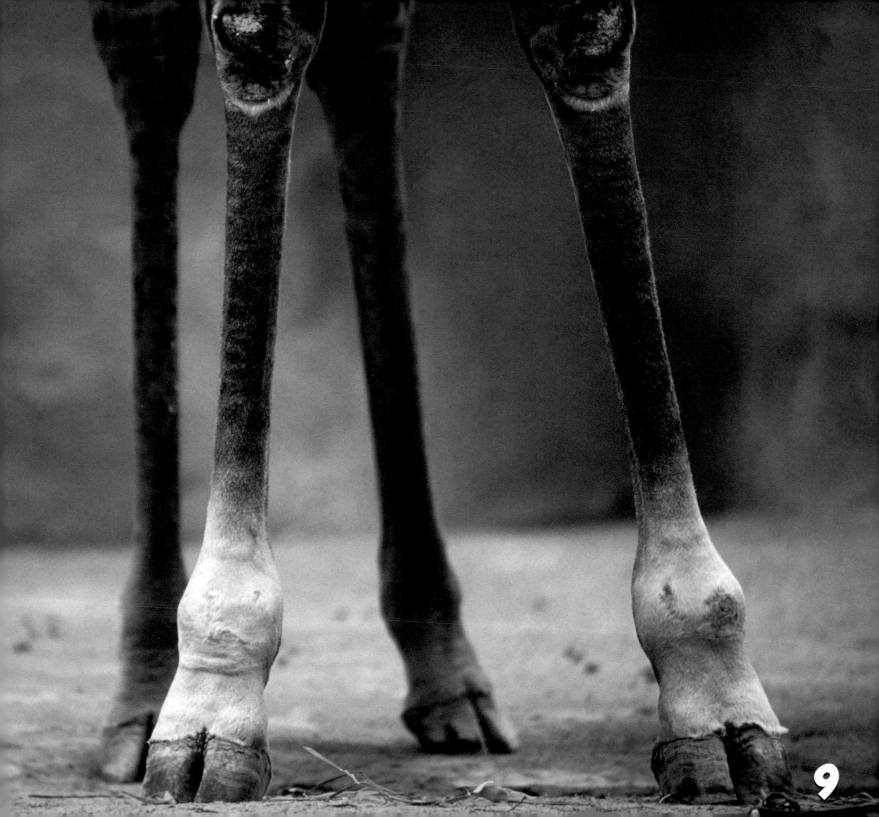

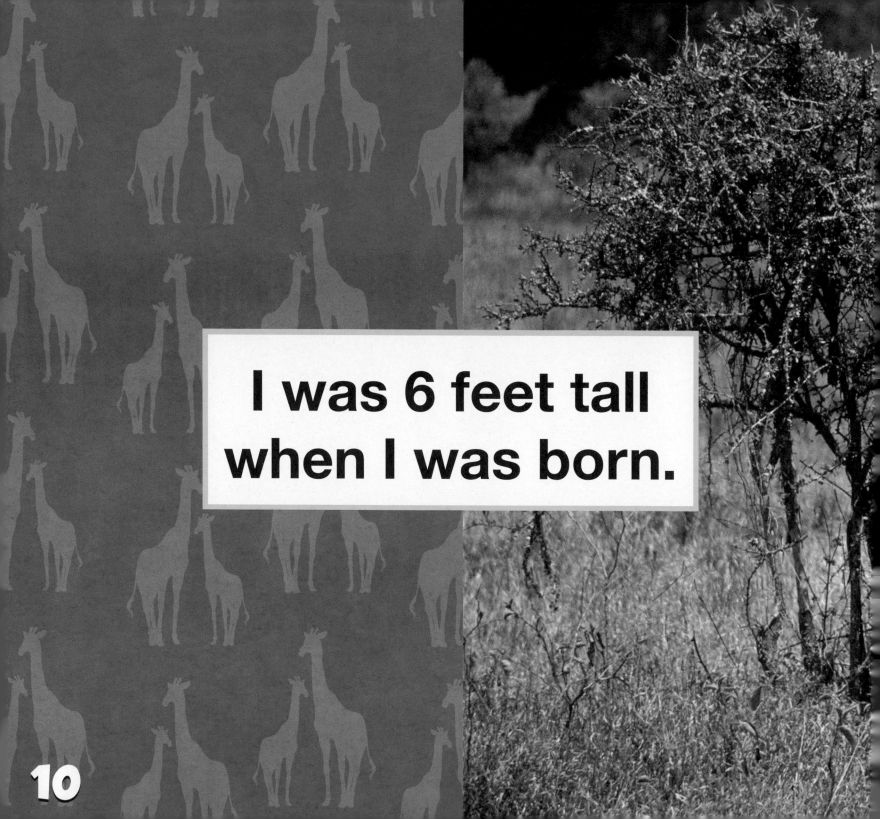

I was 6 feet tall
when I was born.

11

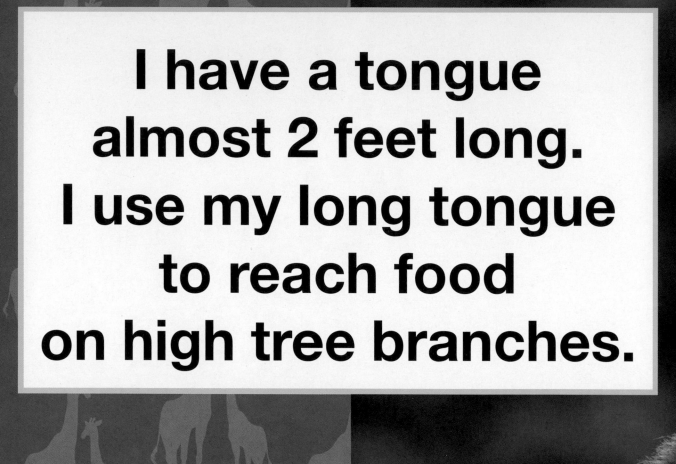

I have a tongue
almost 2 feet long.
I use my long tongue
to reach food
on high tree branches.

13

I can eat up to 145 pounds of food in one day.

14

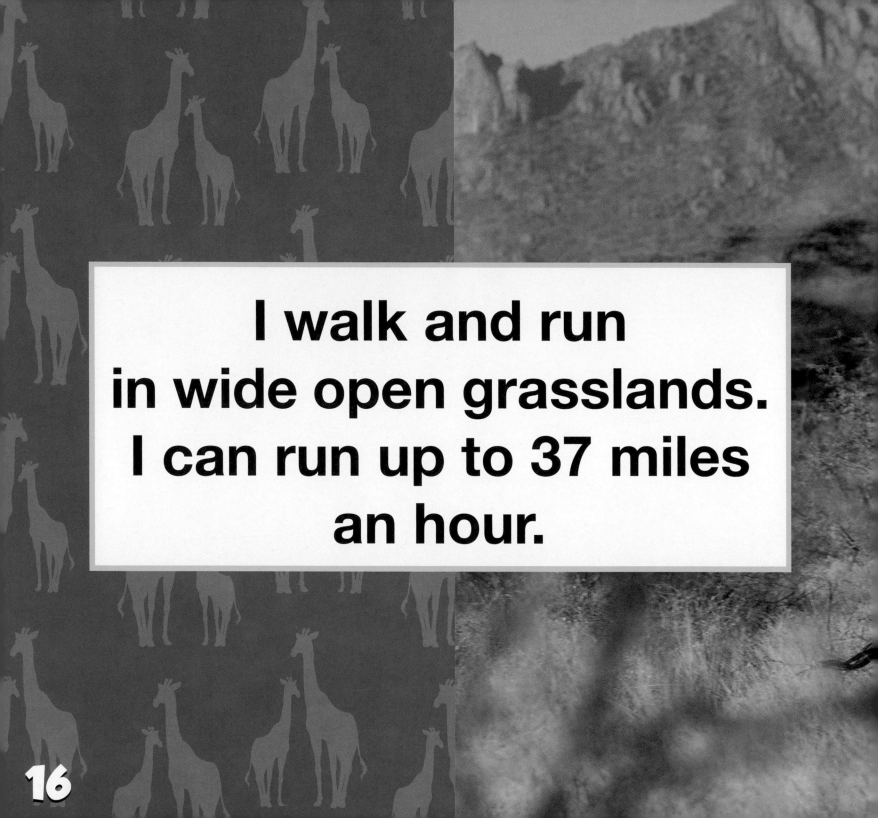

I walk and run
in wide open grasslands.
I can run up to 37 miles
an hour.

I live in a group
with many other giraffes.

I live in a special park where I am safe.

I am a giraffe.

GIRAFFE FACTS

These pages provide detailed information that expands on the interesting facts found in the book. They are intended to be used by adults as a learning support to help young readers round out their knowledge of each amazing animal featured in the *I Am* series.

Pages 4–5

I am a giraffe. There are nine subspecies of giraffe, but scientists now believe some of those may be distinct species of their own. Giraffes are known for their patterned fur. No two have exactly the same fur pattern.

Pages 6–7

I am the tallest animal in the world. The giraffe is best known for its long neck and tall stature. Its neck alone can be up to 6 feet (1.8 meters) long and weigh about 600 pounds (272 kilograms). The largest giraffes can grow up to 19 feet (6 m) tall and weigh more than 4,000 pounds (1,814 kg).

Pages 8–9

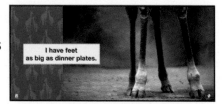

I have feet as big as dinner plates. Their hoofs can be up to 12 inches (30 centimeters) wide. They help spread the giraffe's weight over a larger area. They are also used for defense. A giraffe's legs are about 6 feet (1.8 m) tall. Giraffes walk by moving both legs on one side at the same time, to prevent tangling.

Pages 10–11

I was 6 feet (1.8 m) tall when I was born. Giraffe mothers give birth standing up. The calf may fall up to 6 feet (1.8 m) to the ground when it is born. Calves can weigh up to 220 pounds (100 kg) at birth. The calf and mother stay together for the first week to learn each other's scent.

Pages 12–13

I have a tongue almost 2 feet (0.6 m) long. The giraffe has a prehensile tongue. This means a giraffe can use its tongue like a hand to grasp objects. The tongue is also sticky, allowing the giraffe to easily pick leaves and fruit from high tree branches.

Pages 14–15

I can eat up to 145 pounds (65 kg) of food in one day. Giraffes are herbivores. Their favorite food is the leaves from the acacia tree. Giraffes get most of their water through their food. When they do drink, they must spread their legs far apart and bend their long necks down to reach the water.

Pages 16–17

I walk and run in wide open grasslands. Giraffes can run up to 37 miles (60 kilometers) an hour, for short bursts. They can run for extended periods at speeds up to 31 miles (50 km) per hour. When running, no two hoofs touch the ground at the same time.

Pages 18–19

I live in a group with many other giraffes. Giraffe herds vary. Some are all male. Others are all female. Still others may be a mix of both. Giraffe herds wander freely through an area called their home range. The home range can be as small as 33 square miles (85 square kilometers) or as large as 580 square miles (1,500 sq. km).

Pages 20–21

I live in a special park where I am safe. The giraffe's natural habitat has decreased in size over the past several decades. In 1999, there were about 140,000 giraffes in Africa. Today, there are about 80,000, many of which live on protected wildlife reserves. The West African giraffe and the Rothschild giraffe are both endangered species.

KEY WORDS

Research has shown that as much as 65 percent of all written material published in English is made up of 300 words. These 300 words cannot be taught using pictures or learned by sounding them out. They must be recognized by sight. This book contains 38 common sight words to help young readers improve their reading fluency and comprehension. This book also teaches young readers several important content words, such as proper nouns. These words are paired with pictures to aid in learning and improve understanding.

Page	Sight Words First Appearance
4	a, am, I
6	animal, in, the, world
8	as, big, feet, have
10	was, when
12	almost, food, high, long, my, on, tree, to, use
14	can, eat, day, of, one, up
16	an, and, miles, open, run
18	group, live, many, other, with
20	where

Page	Content Words First Appearance
4	giraffe
8	dinner, plates
12	branches, tongue
14	pounds
16	grasslands, hour
20	park

24